Out of the Mind and into the Heart:

Our Spiritual Journey with Mary Magdalene

By Eileen McCourt

Out of the Mind and into the Heart:

Our Spiritual Journey with Mary Magdalene

By Eileen McCourt

Out of the Mind and into the Heart: Our Spiritual Journey with Mary Magdalene. This book was first published in Great Britain in paperback during August 2017.

The moral right of Eileen McCourt is to be identified as the author of this work and has been asserted by her in accordance with the Copyright, Designs and Patents Act of 1988.

All rights are reserved and no part of this book may be produced or utilized in any format, or by any means, electronic or mechanical, including photocopying, recording or by any information storage or retrieval system, without prior permission in writing from the publishers – Coast & Country/Ads2life. ads2life@btinternet.com

All rights reserved.

ISBN-13: 9781974457229

Copyright © August 2017 Eileen McCourt

CONTENTS

	Page
About the Author	i
Note to reader	v
Acknowledgements	vi
Reviews	vii
Foreword	ix

Chapter 1:	Come back into your heart	1
Chapter 2:	Come back into your body	11
Chapter 3:	Come back into Oneness	16
Chapter 4:	Come back into the Here and Now	25
Chapter 5:	Come back into Trust	29
Chapter 6:	Come back into Truth	35
Chapter 7:	Come back into your inner Goddess	41
Chapter 8:	Come back into Nature	43
Chapter 9:	Come back into your own Spiritual Light	47
Chapter 10:	Come back into Love	49
Chapter 11:	Return of the Goddess	53

CONCLUSION:
From my Heart to Yours: Live your life with passion 67

ABOUT THE AUTHOR

Eileen McCourt is a retired school teacher of English and History with a Master's degree in History from University College Dublin.

She is also a Reiki Grand Master teacher and practitioner, having qualified in Ireland, England and Spain, and has introduced many of the newer modalities of Reiki healing energy into Ireland for the first time, from Spain and England. Eileen has qualified in England through the Lynda Bourne School of Enlightenment, and in Spain through the Spanish Federation of Reiki with Alessandra Rossin, Bienstar, Santa Eulalia, Ibiza.

Regular workshops and healing sessions are held in Elysium Wellness, Newry, County Down; New Moon Holistics N.I. Carrickfergus, County Antrim, and Angel Times Limerick, where Eileen teaches all of the following to both practitioner and teacher levels:

- **Tibetan Usui Reiki levels 1, 2, 3, 4 and Grand Master**
- **Tera-Mai Reiki Seichem**
- **Okuna Reiki (Atlantean and Lemurian)**
- **Reiki Karuna (Indian)**
- **Rahanni Celestial Healing**
- **Fire Spirit Reiki (Christ Consciousness and Holy Spirit)**
- **Mother Mary Reiki**
- **Mary Magdalene Reiki**
- **Archangels Reiki**

- Archangel Ascended Master Reiki
- Violet Flame Reiki
- Lemurian Crystal Reiki
- Golden Eagle Reiki (Native North American Indian)
- Golden Chalice Reiki
- Golden Rainbow Ray Reiki
- Goddesses of Light Reiki
- Unicorn Reiki
- Pegasus Reiki
- Elementals Reiki
- Dragon Reiki
- Dolphin Reiki
- Pyramid of Goddess Isis Reiki
- Magnified Healing of the God Most High of the Universe
- Psychic Surgery

This is Eileen's twelfth book.

Previous publications include:

- **'Living the Magic'**, published in December 2014

- **'This Great Awakening'**, September 2015

- **'Spirit Calling! Are You Listening?'**, January 2016

- **'Working With Spirit: A World of Healing'**, January 2016

- **'Life's But A Game! Go With The Flow!'**, March 2016

- **'Rainbows, Angels and Unicorns!'**, April 2016

- **'........And That's The Gospel Truth!'**, September 2016

- **'The Almost Immaculate Deception! The Greatest Scam in History?'**, September 2016

- **'Are Ye Not Gods?' The true inner meanings of Jesus' teachings and messages'**, March 2017

- **'Jesus Lost and Found'**, July 2017

- **'Behind Every Great Man........ Mary Magdalene Twin Flame of Jesus'**, July 2017

Eileen has also recorded 6 guided meditation cds with her brother, pianist Pat McCourt:

- **'Celestial Healing'**
- **'Celestial Presence'**
- **'Cleansing, energising and balancing the Chakras'**
- **'Ethereal Spirit'**
- **'Open the Door to Archangel Michael'**
- **'Healing with Archangel Raphael'**

All publications are available from Amazon online and all publications and cds are in Angel and Holistic centres around the country, as specified on website.

Website: www.celestialhealing8.co.uk

> **New DVD out in the autumn, 'Living the Magic' in which Eileen gives a general account of what it's like to literally Live the Magic. She discusses excerpts from her 12 books and the contents of her cds.**

Note to reader

This book has materialised very quickly after my previous book on Mary Magdalene, **'Behind Every Great Man.....Mary Magdalene Twin Flame of Jesus'**. This book is different in that it is not about the life of Mary Magdalene, but about her messages to us in these troubled times in which we now find ourselves.

As with all the other books published in my name, I hesitate to claim this most recent one as my own doing. I see myself simply as the tool, the channel, the conduit through which some greater Intelligence is flowing. All I can say is that the information is suddenly in my head and flowing out through the written words. I am not in control of what is happening, I just go with the flow.

Throughout this book, I have mostly used the name **Yeshua** for the person known to us as **Jesus**, for the simple reason that it was as **Yeshua** that Mary Magdalene knew him during their life together 2,000 years ago on this earth dimension.

ACKNOWLEDGEMENTS

I wish to thank, yet again, my publishers, Don Hale OBE and Dr. Steve Green for their advice and input.

And my sincere thanks, yet again, to my family and my wonderful friends for their constant support and encouragement.

Sincere and heart-felt appreciation to all of you who are buying my books and cds and for your kind comments. I am just happy that my books are helping you on your Spiritual path!

Thank you to all who attend my workshops and courses, and to all who have taken the time to write reviews for me, both in my books and on Amazon. You are greatly appreciated!

And as always, I give thanks for all the great blessings that are constantly being sent our way in this wonderful, loving, abundant Universe.

Peace be with you!

Eileen McCourt

REVIEWS

The 17th century mathematician, physicist, inventor, writer and theologian Blaise Pascal commented that "The heart has its reasons of which reason knows nothing."

21st century researchers are increasingly showing that the heart controls the brain much more than previously thought. They have also established that activity in one person's heart can be measured in the brain waves of another person.

It is opportune therefore that this latest offering from McCourt should choose to focus its message on the importance of listening to and living from the heart.

Drawing heavily on Jungian Psychology and the animus/anima, male/female dichotomy, this book yet again advances the thesis that the old male dominated order is redundant, and indeed, repugnant and meaningless in our modern world.

As Jung himself said, "Your vision will become clear only when you can look into your own heart. Who looks outside, dreams; who looks inside awakes".

P.McC   Psychologist

This a lovely book full of divine wisdom and advice.

Over the years most of us have loosened our belief on the spiritual aspects of life. We have chosen to live from our heads totally rather than our hearts. What is the difference? When we live from our hearts we live from a place of pure love. From this 'place' we can receive much needed guidance and care.

Living from our hearts also means that we take back our 'power'. Spiritual power is aligning ourselves with the Divine within us all. As we receive and act on the heart advice, we soften our energy. We begin to realise that there is a more loving way to live. We loosen our grip on the materialistic, ego driven world. But we do this in a way that is soft and joyful.

Our Divine essence can guide us to what is best for our highest good. There is no one solution that fits all souls. Divine guidance is individual and very precious.

For some readers, the material in this book will be familiar and perhaps forgotten. For others, this book is just what they needed to know. Their soul will have guided them to read the book. Either way, the reader will come back to this book many times as they begin to open their minds to a better, more loving way to experience life on this beautiful planet.

There is a lot of information to process. It is a very individualised learning experience. Some may read it in one sitting. Others may read a bit of the book, put it down and allow the data to sit with them to allow for a greater understanding.

KMA

A beautiful book which must be published.

This book contains many gemstones of spiritual advice for the novice and the more advanced. Keep a copy close at hand - its references of channelled writings of MARY Magdalene to follow the spiritual path are detailed, knowledgeable, simplistic yet *astounding*.

Clare Bowman

Foreword

Mary Magdalene's time has finally come! After 1,500 years of defamation and castigation as a sinner and a prostitute, the veils surrounding her are lifting, revealing a much-maligned woman. A woman who is now taking her rightful place, a woman who was a teacher, a visionary, an emissary of the Light, a remarkably strong, independent disciple of Jesus, a woman who explained Jesus' teachings to the other disciples, the '*apostle to the apostles*', well qualified to be Jesus' Spiritual partner and his rightful successor in spreading the teachings of '*The Way*'.

Scorned and ostracized for simply being a woman, her situation exacerbated not only for being a woman, but because she was a powerful woman, a priestess trained in the Temple of Isis in Egypt, she fought her ground against all the odds, supporting and teaching alongside Jesus, his '*Tower*', his main support mechanism, the only disciple left at the cross when most of the others had fled.

This book is not about the life of Mary Magdalene. There are sufficient books out there now which show us beyond any doubt that she was the close companion of Jesus, his constant support, his sexual partner, and who knows, perhaps even his wife and the mother of his child or children. So this book is different. This book, following closely on the heels of my previous book on Mary Magdalene, **'Behind Every Great Man.... Mary Magdalene, Twin Flame of Jesus',** is about her profound messages of love, hope and compassion, messages intended to change our ways of thinking and move us further upwards and onwards on our Spiritual path of soul evolution, raising our own soul consciousness and the collective soul awareness of all humanity.

It is Mary Magdalene the Spiritual teacher, Mary Magdalene the loving, understanding, supportive, compassionate friend, who now speaks to us through the pages of this book, urging us, guiding us along our own Spiritual path, doing for us what she did for the other disciples, as she puts the teachings of Jesus into simpler terms, lighting up the path for us, awakening us to a deeper understanding of who and what we are, and most importantly, where exactly we are heading on our long walk-about across eternity.

Mary Magdalene's strong, passionate and compassionate energy gushes out of these pages, inviting the reader to come with her, inviting the reader to be guided by her, inviting the reader to develop a personal relationship with her, as she promises to lead us out of the world of illusion and bring us to a deeper understanding of reality. She represents the Divine Feminine, and in her partnership with Yeshua, together they expressed the totality of Oneness in the joining of the Divine Feminine and the Divine Masculine, Mary herself being the more earthy one, complementing Yeshua, the more out-of-the-ordinary.

This is what we are all aiming for, merging our masculine and feminine aspects, becoming complete, perfected, enjoying life from living in the wholeness of the Oneness rather than existing in the limitation of merely one or the other. As above, so below. Our union of the feminine and masculine within each one of us here on the earth plane reflects the union of Father/Mother God in the totality of All THAT IS.

Let Mary, through this book, guide you to a life lived with passion, through and from your heart, which in turn generates happiness, joy and meaning. Only by living life in such a way can we allow our inner Spiritual Light to shine forth to all. Only by living life with passion and hence with happiness, joy and meaning can we advance our soul on this, our present earthly journey, just one of our many life-time journeys throughout eternity.

As Mary joins us now, see her enter, her flaming auburn hair flowing loosely, gently and gracefully down over her shoulders, her scarlet and gold robe moving softly in the delicate breeze, her soulful deep eyes emitting love and compassion, as she greets us and gently gathers us to her. Let us listen, at her feet, to her profound words of wisdom and guidance, intermingled with snippets from her own life with Yeshua 2,000 years ago, as she delivers her message to us, words which she has patiently waited 2,000 years to deliver, to deliver to those who are ready and willing to listen and to hear.

Let us hear the voice of a Master.

Let us listen to the words of Ascended Master Mary Magdalene.

Eileen McCourt

16th August 2017

CHAPTER 1:

COME BACK INTO YOUR HEART

Greetings! Peace be with you all! I bring you Love and Light!

I am Mary of Magdala, best known to you as Mary Magdalene, so it is as Mary Magdalene that I now come to you. I am from the higher echelons of the Spirit world, the highest of Spiritual dimensions where all is Love and Light.

I am coming to you now, on your earth vibration, because the time has now come. How I have waited so patiently for this time! The time to reinstate the divine feminine to its rightful place, the time to restore the balance between the divine masculine and the divine feminine which have been out of balance for the last 2,000 years, the time to restore wholeness and harmony to your world which has suffered so much as a result of that imbalance.

A new age is dawning, a new age where the divine feminine will once again rise to the fore, healing the deep wounds of separation, separation from Oneness and wholeness, leading to the end of individualism and a re-uniting of All That Is.

This is not any sort of competition or any sort of attempt at a reversal of fortunes! This is no battle of the sexes! This is not any sort of attempt at getting even! Or any attempt on the part of the feminine to oust the masculine and attain dominance! Not at all! This is a merging, a combining, a uniting of the divine masculine and the divine feminine into the Oneness, into the Wholeness of Completion. For the last 2,000 years, the masculine has been allowed to dominate, and the result has been a fractious world, a warring world, a warring world which threatens to destroy your entire universe. That will not be allowed to happen. There are too many extra-terrestrial beings watching, beyond your human sight or sensory mechanisms, who have only your earth's best interests at heart.

While the masculine has been in control, humanity has been living in and through the mind, and particularly in the lower mind, that which you call the ego. The heart, the divine feminine, has been isolated, excluded, cut off, superimposed upon by a dominant, controlling, aggressively competitive masculine energy.

It is time now for the merging, the marriage of the sacred masculine mind, and the sacred feminine heart, to bring about the new age for which humanity has been waiting for so long.

And I am here to assist you all in bringing about that merging of your sacred mind and your sacred heart, your divine masculine and your divine feminine. I am here to assist in the lifting of the mists and the veils that have clouded your sacred mind for so long, and to show you how to live through the union of your heart and your sacred mind, creating a love-filled, compassionate and transformed world, where you are all once again restored to living through the beautiful expression of your own sexuality, your own inherent feelings, your own emotions. For all of these, truth, love and compassion come from the heart, but the heart has been closed down for so long now, that humanity has forgotten what it is to live from the heart, to live in your feelings and emotions generated by your own feeling, loving heart.

As a young girl, when I lived on earth 2,000 years ago, I was taught by my mother to see divinity in every living form. Absolutely everything you see or experience is the manifestation of the creativity of the great Universal God energy. And when you acknowledge and accept that divine creativity in everything around you, allowing yourself to feel the emotions and feelings generated naturally in your own self, and not reacting from the dictates of others, then you are living from your heart.

Returning to living from the heart is what humanity needs to do. Returning to the divine feminine, and hence to living from the heart is what I want to help you achieve.

Your heart is your mechanism, your channel, your conduit, through which you receive and transmit divine Love and Light. Your heart now needs to be opened and activated again, after being dormant and closed for so long. And your emotions, your feelings, your sexuality all come from and through your heart. So by existing with a closed heart, you have been denying your own inherent emotions and feelings and your own sacred sexuality. You have given your power away, the power of your heart, the power of your heart to generate those same inherent feelings and emotions which are the very fabric of life. Those same inherent feelings and emotions which are the great sign posts, the great informers, the great guides on the journey of your soul. Get to recognise and know your own inherent feelings and what they represent on your soul journey.

You are not a robot, but you have been existing like one. You have not been living! Your strings of life have been pulled, just like a puppet. Your mind has been taken over at the expense of your heart! You are living like a computer, programmed for everything you do. But you are not a computer! A computer has no heart. Computers have taken over your lives. This is the masculine energy which has been allowed to dominate. How often have you said, in exasperation, '*this computer of mine has a mind of its own*'? But you never say '*this computer of mine has a heart of its own*'! That's because it has no heart! That's because you yourself know that it has no heart! A computer cannot feel, a computer cannot show emotions, simply because it has no mechanism through which it can display or register feelings and emotions. It has no heart. But **you** have a heart!

Those who would control you know the power of emotions and the great power that emotions generate. Generated and organised emotions can topple governments and all sorts of institutions. That's why you have been taught to deny and suppress your feelings and emotions. They are dangerous for those who seek to control you, and you are easy to control when you are cut off from your real power, when you are cut off from the real power of your emotions. When you are living from your controlled and programmed mind and not from your heart, that means that you have stifled your natural feelings and emotions, the essential and vital pathways of connection to your heart. Your mind has become controlled by external manipulators, for their own devious ends, but your emotions and feelings are generated from within yourself. And anything coming from within yourself does not lie, manipulate or deceive you.

Out of The Mind and Into The Heart

Your emotions are therefore divine aspects of yourself, states of pure feeling. However, often you confuse your emotions with judgements, when you feel shame, guilt, anger or whatever. These are not true feelings, true feelings coming from your heart, for remember, your heart in its pure form knows only truth, unconditional love and compassion. Truth, unconditional love and compassion come from Source, so your heart leads you back to Source.

It is time now to get out of your mind and back again into your heart, into living your life as it should be lived, through your feelings and emotions, and not through the clouded vision which your mind has become. It is time to release your heart from the stifling and suffocating control of your mind, and to feel the freedom of the enjoyment of life that you will feel when you live through your heart, and by living through your heart, you will be returning not only yourself to balance, but the whole of your suffering world.

Picture your entire life as your own special creation, work of art or painting. To paint, you need a canvas. Your heart is that canvas, the canvas on which you paint your life. To paint, you need paint. Love is the paint with which you paint your life painting. To paint, you need a paint brush. Conviction, or indeed passion, is the brush with which you paint your life painting. To paint, you need inspiration. Meditation generates the inspiration for your life painting. And the result? A work of art that reflects your own unique consciousness. A beautiful work of art that you have painted on the canvas of your heart! A beautiful work of art that you have produced with no interference from your controlled mind! A mind that has been controlled by so many influences outside of yourself.

Sadly, most people do not even know how to live by the heart any more. Living by the mind has taken over. So what is the difference between living through the mind and living through the heart?

Living through the heart simply means allowing yourself to experience and feel all the emotions which constantly arise through your daily life. Allow them to come to the surface and acknowledge them, because they come from the heart. And not just allowing yourself to experience them, but also to allow yourself to integrate these feelings and emotions into your resultant output back to the world again. In other words, your actions must come from your own inherent emotions and feelings, which in turn are generated by your heart. Remember, your heart, when left to its own devices, and not super-imposed upon by the mind, knows only truth, unconditional love and compassion.

Your lower mind, on the other hand, is coming mostly from your ego, from what you have been conditioned into believing and doing. Ever since you were a young child, your lower mind has been conditioned in all sorts of ways, as you were trained how to behave, how to do everything, how to do what was expected of you by your parents, by your teachers, by society. And now in the work force, you are still doing what is expected of you by your employers, and of course, by the norms of society. Nothing needs to be learned at the level of the mind. That is merely your ego. Your ego, your mind, is just too smart for your own good. It analyses everything, tearing everything apart, suggesting this, suggesting that, talking and chattering away, busy, busy, busy, imposing its own will on you, making you feel fear and guilt. Your mind is constantly thinking, processing the energy of thoughts. But it is your heart that experiences feelings. It is your heart, not your mind that is your connection to Source. You cannot be connected to Source if and when you are living through your mind. When you are not in your mind, you are in **Oneness.** God is love, and you cannot feel love with your mind, only with your heart. So therefore you can feel God only with your heart.

Yes, the functions of your lower mind are essential, but it is when they start to overrule your heart that they become a problem. Your lower mind and your feeling heart must work together, with your heart taking precedence. If you are not allowing your heart to feel, and if you are not taking cognizance of those feelings, you are disconnected from the natural world, with its natural cycles and rhythms, simply because your heart beats in tandem with the natural cycles and rhythms of the natural world. It is from your heart that you learn wisdom and knowledge. Wisdom and knowledge are not to be found in the mind.

Take for example, the times at which you eat. Do you follow the natural feelings coming from your heart telling you that you are hungry, or do you follow what your lower mind tells you, what your mechanised watch on your wrist is telling your mind, that it is now a certain time, time to eat? Do you eat by the clock or by your own feelings of hunger? Are you controlled by time or are you in control of the time allotted to you for this life-time?

Another name for your lower mind is your ego, which has clouded your higher or sacred mind. You must re-connect with your higher mind, that part of your mind that gives you inspiration, connection to Source, awareness, insight and psychic powers. Your sacred mind can only be accessed through meditation. You must learn to unite and use your masculine sacred mind and your feeling feminine heart.

Living through your lower mind means denying your own inherent feelings and emotions and living according to the dictates of society, trading your own inherent intuitive mechanism system, your own inherent wisdom, for the rules and regulations, the standards and codes of practice imposed by other outside influences and authorities.

The uniting of your higher, sacred mind and your feminine sacred heart is the sacred marriage, and it is through this sacred marriage of your mind and your heart that you receive Love and Light into your thirsty, gasping soul and into your physical body. You can draw Light into yourself through your sacred higher mind, let it merge with the Love from your feeling beautiful heart, and circulate this powerful Love-Light all through your own body and out into the world.

Let me teach you a simple exercise to do this! An exercise that will show you how easily you can create Love-Light for yourself and for your world! Love-Light that will transmute the negativity and darkness that is so prevalent in your world today!

You can do this simple exercise during meditation, when you are grounding, or in a few seconds if you are in a hurry.

Be still. Breathe in deeply, drawing in the divine feminine love, the light and energy from Mother Earth up through your lower chakras and into your heart. Feel that divine feminine love from Mother

Earth filling your body, holding you, supporting you. *Feel this divine feminine love in your heart.* Now draw the divine masculine light from the sun, the heavens, the celestial kingdoms, down through your crown chakra, your third eye, your throat chakra and down into your heart. *Feel this divine masculine light in your heart. Let this divine masculine light from above now merge with the divine feminine love in your heart, spiralling out through your body, out through your aura, and from there out into the world.* This is all you have to do! This is all you have to do to send Love and Light out into your world. Your world that is gasping, crying out desperately for Love and Light!

Look in your heart, dear ones! It is only in your heart that you can connect with your own God essence. Master your mind, your ego, and rule your life! Master your mind and free your heart! Master your mind and transform your world! It is only when your world gets to a no-mind level of being that heaven can come on earth. It is only when you can get to a level of consciousness where you do no-thing that you can calm and quiet your mind, cutting off its constant, relentless thoughts and chatter, allowing you to connect with your divine essence. It is only when humanity ends the search for God outside of themselves, which is ego-driven, and looks within, looks within to the heart, that your world will evolve. The mind in your world is now running rampant, out of control! Mind madness rules! Ego dictatorship! Love needs to return to your world! Humanity needs to freely choose to act from a place of love rather than from the erstwhile destructive, debilitating place of the ego!

One of the greatest Spiritual teachers who incarnated on your earth was Buddha. Like Yeshua and like all the ancient masters, Buddha also taught that your mind needs to be controlled in order to prevent it controlling you. Let me remind you of some of the words of Buddha:

'You must first discipline and control your own mind. If a man can control his mind he can find the way to Enlightenment, and all virtue and wisdom will naturally be his'.

Everything changes constantly in you except the beat of your heart. Listen to your heart! Live from your heart! Let your heart take precedence over your mind! Let your mind go and let yourself be in the present! Open your heart! Follow your heart and live a truly fulfilled life!

With Love and Light!

I AM Mary Magdalene.

CHAPTER 2:

COME BACK INTO YOUR BODY

DEAR ONES!

I bring you Love and Light!

You are a beautiful Spiritual being, a beautiful soul shining your light out to all others! Your physical body is the temple for your beautiful, magnificent soul. A temple is always a place of beauty, the house or casing for the beauty, grace and majesty that lies within.

Temples are seen throughout your entire world as places of beauty, serenity and majesty, places admired and respected simply because of their inner content. Temples cared for and looked after out of respect and love for what lies within. Your own physical body is the temple for your beautiful soul, yet you do not give it the same respect or admiration that you would give to other temples. You do not care for your temple, your beautiful sacred body in the same way other temples are cared for.

Your body is beautiful. A beautiful temple for your soul. A beautiful sacred temple, a beautiful manifestation of the hand of God. Your sexuality is sacred. Your sexuality is the manifestation of the creativity of the great universal God energy. Sacred too, because it creates life. But you do not seem to realise this!

A rose is beautiful. You admire a rose. All flowers are beautiful. You admire all flowers. You admire the colours of Autumn, the ocean, the beauty of a fading sunset, the grandeur and magnificence of the rising sun, the glory and majesty of the mountains, the hand of God manifested everywhere in Mother Nature and in all forms of life. By admiring them you are admiring Mother Nature, seeing the hand of God manifested everywhere. You love and care for your pet, stroking, cuddling, fondling, nurturing, showering it with love and affection.

But your own sacred body! Your own sacred body, equally a manifestation of the creativity of the great universal energy that is God! Many of you despise and hate your body! Many of you are ashamed of your body, seeing it as ugly, too thin, too fat, too this, too that, too whatever. Many of you do not see the beauty of your sexuality! Many of you see your sexuality as shameful, sinful even. But your sexuality is the creator of life! Many of you fail to see your body for what it really is! A beautiful, wonderful manifestation of Father/Mother God. The body that you yourself designed exclusively for yourself before you incarnated on the earth plane. The body that you yourself co-created with Father/Mother God to transport you through your current life as you learn the lessons you yourself decided to learn in order to evolve your beautiful soul.

So many of you live outside your body. So many of you live completely detached from your body. So many of you abuse your body through drugs, alcohol and other toxic substances. Many of you have been taught not to touch your body, but all parts of your body are beautiful, and touching your own body is the greatest therapy, bringing it alive as you caress it with love and affection.

Out of The Mind and Into The Heart

Your body heals through your own loving touch, responding to the positive energy generated by your feelings, which you transmit into it. Similarly, when you send messages to your body through your thoughts or feelings of shame or repulsion, then your body reacts by becoming disconnected from you, becoming literally out of touch with you.

It saddens us greatly on the other side of the veil to see so many of you so completely out of touch with your body and your body's needs. Your magnificent, amazing, wonderful body! And it saddens us also to see how so many of you feel ashamed of your sexuality. But your sexuality is all about your union with the Divine. The sacred sexual act is all about uniting the masculine and the feminine into One.

How can any act that creates life be considered vulgar and indecent? But that is what your Christian Church has declared the sacred sexual act to be. Vulgar! Vile! Revolting! And as a result, the beautiful sacred sexual act has become debased, misused, deflowered, violated and exploited for mercenary and lustful means.

Your emotions and feelings generate energy. The sacred sexual act is the uniting of the masculine and the feminine into One. And when that sacred sexual act is undertaken with respect and love, the energy generated by the feelings and emotions generates the strongest, the most potent energy the human body can manufacture. I tell you this, dear ones, because I was a priestess in the Temple of Isis in Egypt during my lifetime as Mary Magdalene 2,000 years ago, where the practice of sexual alchemy was well understood and respected. The sacred sexual act, when practised with a partner was known then as the Sex Magic of Isis, or, if practised alone, as the Alchemy of Horus. The true function of sexuality, the union of the masculine and the feminine was seen as union with the divine, a deeply Spiritual experience, opening to the Higher Self and the higher Spiritual realms. Today, this sacred sex is still practised in your Eastern religions, in India, for example, in the Hindu religion, where it is known as Tantric yoga or Kundalini yoga. The sacred sexual act for most of you now has become merely an act of pleasure, a quick, satisfying, fulfilling release of tension. But for yogis and yoginis it is much more than that. It is a raising of Spiritual consciousness, a heightened state of awareness that strengthens one's connection to the divine. This is a natural state of heightened consciousness that your body can attain through the natural sacred sexual act. But unfortunately, because it has been debased so much, and because you have never been taught about this, most of you seek to attain a heightened state of consciousness through drugs and other abusive substances.

My dear ones, you need to re-connect with your body and your own sexuality. You need to start loving and nurturing your beautiful body, seeing it as the temple of your shining immortal soul. You need to start loving your body.

Loving your body and loving yourself does not mean indulging yourself in material goods. That is only transitory false satisfaction, temporary false comfort. Loving your body means loving being you, being happy in your own skin. Loving yourself means seeing yourself as the beautiful bright shining Spiritual light you really are. Loving yourself means not judging yourself, not harbouring feelings of guilt, not beating yourself up over something you have or have not done. Loving yourself means accepting yourself exactly as you are, here and now. All that is on the surface is false. The beauty lies beneath. It is the soul light that shines out, not the body. Nothing is ever what it seems on the surface.

Loving your body, loving being in your own skin, loving being you, embracing and enjoying your sexuality, embracing the sacred sexual act and sexual energy as a uniting with the divine, leads you to a state of wholeness within your own self, which in turn opens the doorways to your Spiritual growth in the higher realms.

With Love and Light!

I AM Mary Magdalene.

CHAPTER 3:

COME BACK INTO ONENESS

My dear ones!

Love and Light!

We are all **One**. There is no separation. We are all **One** with each other and we are all **One** in the great vastness of the Universal God Energy. Everything in the entirety and totality of creation is incorporated into **Oneness**. Realising and acknowledging this **Oneness** underpins all Spiritual understanding. Accepting this **Oneness**, and living in this **Oneness** is the first step on the path of your Spiritual and soul evolution.

Oneness is your natural state of being, dear ones. **Oneness** is your deepest self, your deepest roots, your source, your ultimate connection to **All That Is**. **Oneness** is you in your purest essence. **Oneness** cannot be attained by contemplating something that is outside of yourself and trying to make it yours. It is only your ego that keeps telling your mind that you are separate, that you are an individual. It is only your ego that keeps you trapped in individualism, living in the limiting power of that individualism rather than in the unlimited potential of living in **Oneness**.

You are in God and God is in you. Many of you do not yet realise this. You spend your time looking for God in all the wrong places. God is not in any place **outside of yourself,** and if you are trying to find God outside of yourself, then you are seeing God as something separate, something apart from yourself. Indeed, even if you are trying to find God **within yourself,** you are still seeing God as a separate entity from yourself, simply because of the very fact that you are looking for God at all, trying to **find God**, whether outside or inside of yourself. You do not have to look for God or **find God** anywhere at all! And why not? Because **you already are** God!

Being God is not just a belief! **Being God** is not just an idea! That is your mind, your ego talking to you. Your ego comes from fear. Fear that you will lose yourself, your individuality, in the **Oneness of All**. Fear that you will be swallowed up, annihilated. And so you hold onto your individualism and separateness in order to protect yourself. Be with that fear whenever it arises. Do not judge yourself, stay in the present moment so that your mind does not start to analyse or intellectualize it. Perceiving separation is what has caused your world to be in the sorry state in which it now is.

Being God is an experience! **Being God** is a living, on-going, infinite experience! **Being God** is reality! **Being God** is all there is! To experience **Being God** requires practice and discipline. And that does not mean practice and discipline of the mind or body. Rather, it means living in the presence, the presence of your heart, your connection to Source, the presence of your soul, surrendering your own will completely and totally, relaxing into the **Oneness.** Your heart that beats in tandem with the pulse, the heart beat of all creation! By listening to your heart, and only by listening to your heart, you are living in the **Oneness**.

Let me explain. Think of the vastness of the ocean. Now think of the wave in that vastness of the ocean. The wave is only there because the ocean is there. The ocean gives life to the wave, the ocean contains the wave in its vastness. The wave has no existence outside of the ocean. It cannot exist anywhere else, simply because it is part of the ocean. This same wave builds up to a crest and then crashes. Now it is no longer a wave, but it is still in the ocean. It does not need to look around and see where the ocean has gone or how it can get back into the ocean. The wave *is* the ocean. The wave is not the ocean in its entirety, but it is there, part of it, not apart from it, possessing all the elements of the ocean. It has nowhere else to go! Simply because there is nowhere else that it can have any form of life!

Imagine dipping your finger into the ocean. On your finger now is a tiny droplet of the ocean. That tiny droplet contains all the elements of the ocean, the salty taste, the watery essence, the same substance, but it is not the ocean in its entirety. It came from the ocean, and it can only have life or exist within the ocean.

Can you see what I am saying to you here?

You are a spark of divine essence. **YOU ARE GOD**! You are God in that you carry within yourself all of the elements of Father/Mother God. You exist within the great Universal God Energy because you are part of that great Universal God Energy, not apart from it. You can exist nowhere else, simply because there is nowhere else for you to exist, no more than there is anywhere else for the wave to exist outside of the vastness of the entirety of the ocean.

So, if you are God in that you carry all the elements of Father/Mother God within you, you must begin to see yourself as the magnificent, powerful being you really are. But so many of you limit yourselves because you see yourself as separate from God, searching for God here and there and all over the place, when you yourself are actually of divine essence, the God essence!

Let me give you a powerful exercise which will bring all of this home to you.

This exercise is the powerful *'I AM'* confirmation, the confirmation of divine presence within each one of you. Say to yourself, over and over again:

'I AM THAT I AM THAT I AM'.

'BE STILL AND KNOW THAT I AM GOD'.

The *'I'* in all of this is yourself!

I want you to live in the remembrance of who and what you really are, a spark of divine essence, carrying within you all the elements of the Godhead. Your power is divine, so the only limitations on you are the limitations you yourself impose on yourself.

Now let me take this a step further for you.

If, as I have just explained, you yourself carry all the elements of the Godhead within you, and your power has no limitation, then what happens when you pray? What exactly is prayer?

Most of you see prayer as a request to an external God, somewhere out there, beyond the clouds, an external God who will grant some requests and refuse others. But I have just explained that you yourself are God. This is not blasphemy or Spiritual arrogance! It is just you accepting your own natural inherent divine essence, acknowledging and accepting who and what you really are. It's as simple and straightforward as that!

So if you are of the God essence, then when you pray to God, who are you really praying to? Is it not obvious? Yes, my dear ones, you are praying to yourself! To the God essence that you really are! To your own Higher Self! Your own Higher Self which is the Godhead in you! Your own Higher Self, which, being the Godhead, knows absolutely everything and has all the answers to all the questions you could ever ask! Your own Higher Self which will guide you to the right answer! Your own Higher Self to which you always have access! It is part of you, not separate from you!

And how do you access your own Higher Self?

You can only access your own Higher Self through quiet meditation. You can only access your own Higher Self for the answer to any question through raising your consciousness level above the base consciousness level at which most people operate on a daily basis. Your Higher Self cannot be accessed when you are surrounded by the noise and confusion that bombard you all on a daily basis. You need to extricate yourself from all of that and tune into your own divinity. And the main tool for that is meditation.

Meditation is not just sitting quietly thinking about this or that or whatever. Meditation is sitting quietly, away from all interfering noise or disturbance, listening to the stillness and quiet, and focusing on your own breathing. As you focus on your breathing, and connect with your own breath, you are connecting with Spirit, simply because breath is the transmitter of Spirit. Breath *is* Spirit, Spirit *is* breath. As you continue to breathe, you will begin to feel that you yourself are being breathed in and out by a force greater, more expansive than you. As indeed you are! You, all of you, are being breathed in and out as part of the great **Universal Breath** that is all creation. We are all living through the same pulse that pulsates throughout all creation, the **Oneness** that is entirety, the **Oneness** that is infinity. There is no separation! There is only **Oneness**! And when you feel that Oneness, that sense of being incorporated into the vastness of the **Oneness**, when you feel yourself pulsating in synchronicity with **All That Is**, when you feel yourself beating in rhythm with all of creation, then you have raised your consciousness to a level where you are connecting with the higher energy vibrational energy frequencies that surround us on all sides, all of which we are a part, and not apart from, then you can receive the messages from your own Higher Self, guiding you to the action for the highest good of all. I emphasise for the highest good of all, because we are all one, and you cannot benefit at the expense of anyone else. It is your ego, your lower mind that urges you to '*go for it*' whatever that might be, regardless of how the outcome might affect other people or other forms of life.

So know that you truly are divine beings, powerful Spiritual beings, carrying the balance of Father/Mother God within each of you, divine beings of Light, connected to the **Oneness** of all creation, to the **Oneness** of **All That Is.** It is through connection to your own innate wisdom and inner knowing, and through that only, that you can empower yourself and live your life in peace, serenity and love, secure in your own inner knowledge that you are part of the **Grand Design**, the **Grand Plan** for all of humanity, which in turn is part of the **Grand Design**, the **Grand Plan** for all of creation.

Continue to stay in your '*I AM PRESENCE*', for it is there and there only that you will experience joy and happiness, secure in your knowledge that you are an inherent part of **ALL THAT IS**. Outside of your **'I AM PRESENCE'**, there is only separation, separation from your divine source, separation that drags along with it in its entourage, only suffering, darkness and fear.

Let me show you a simple exercise whereby you yourself can experience, here and now, this inherent natural feeling of **Oneness**.

Sit or stand face to face with your partner or a friend. Extend your left arm outwards and upwards, palm faced upwards, in the receiving position. Now place your right hand on your partner's heart. Feel the heart beat of that person whose heart you are now touching. Now listen to your own heart beat. Feel your two hearts move effortlessly into synchronicity, both beating as one. You are now at **One** with that person. Now try and extend that synchronised heart beating of both your hearts out into the universe and throughout the entire cosmos. Feel the pulse of life in everything all around you beating in tandem with your two already synchronised hearts. Feel the **Oneness**! Feel the heartbeat of the **Oneness** of **All That Is**!

Can you feel that, dear ones? Can you feel that everything pulsates to the same heart beat? Not to the same mind beat, but to the same *heart* beat!

There is only **Oneness**, there is no separation, we are all **One**.

So, as we are all **One**, can you now see that by hurting or destroying any other person or hurting or destroying any other form of life, you are actually hurting or destroying yourself? Yes, you are actually doing this to yourself!

And as we all dwell in **Oneness** then there is the responsibility on every shoulder to care for all that is within that **Oneness**! Humanity must take responsibility for the earth, for the environment, for all forms of life in that environment. And you must all care for each other! There is no point in having abolished slavery and yet continuing to believe that slavery is over if humanity insists on keeping fellow men enslaved in poorly paid labour, in sweated industries, exploiting poorer countries to feed the mercenary greed of the larger corporations and private individuals. There is no point in pushing an agenda, a reform or a belief unless you are prepared to act, to see the situation through the eyes of love, through the eyes of those who are suffering, and to intervene and work ceaselessly on their behalf.

Selfishness, self-centredness, working for oneself and furthering one's own individual agenda is the cause of all the cruelty, exploitation and suffering in your world today. These people see themselves outside of **Oneness**. These people are operating from the mind, the ego. Ego is the greatest of vampires, rampant in your world, constantly sucking from humanity for individual gains, and contributing nothing to humanity in return. You allow ego to take over your lives because it makes you feel better about yourselves. It makes you feel superior to others. But when you live in your ego and allow it to dictate to you, you are living in an unawakened state, in a world of unawareness, in a world of unconsciousness. Unaware of what? Unaware of the connectedness of all life. Unconscious and oblivious to the fact that we are all **One**, all **One** in the vast universal energy that creates and sustains all life. Those of you living in ego seek recognition and rewards for what you do. You see **'Me'**, **'Mine'** and **'My'** as all that is, and hence you are out of alignment, out of balance with the great universal energy flow. Ego tells you that you are separate individuals, in a competitive world, where only the fittest survive.

But remember, my dear ones, what you do to other forms of life, you do to yourself! Simply because everything and everyone is part of the same and only **Oneness**.

So come back into **Oneness**! Drop the ego, recognising it as the imposter it truly is, pretending to be your true nature, your true self, promising you everything, but delivering only short-lived satisfaction and transient happiness. Come back into **Oneness** and find the true joy and true peace that we beyond the veil truly wish for you all to have!

With Love and Light!

I AM Mary Magdalene.

CHAPTER 4:

COME BACK INTO THE HERE AND NOW

My Dear Ones!

Love and Light!

The gift of life is a beautiful, unique present to all of you! And the only place you can ever be is in the '***present***', the '***here and now***'. There is no other place. You talk about the past. But the past is gone! You talk about the future. But the future will never come! You must understand this! When tomorrow comes, it is still the present!

The present is the only place you can ever be!

We in the higher vibrational energy frequencies watch with great sadness how so many of you continue to hold onto your past, holding onto what is now gone! Yes, the past has in many ways made you what you are, but it does not serve your ***present*** life purpose any longer if you continue to try to live there. And what does not serve you, you must discard.

Living in the present means really being fully aware of everything around you at this moment in time. Living in this moment in time heightens and sharpens all of your senses. Living in this one moment makes you come alive, enables you to live with passion in the joys and delights unfolding all around you! Living in this one moment opens you to all of this! But most of you are oblivious to all the wonders and joys around you, simply because you are not where you should be, you are not in the here and now.

You are all on a journey. You are all on a journey back to Light. And you will all reach your destination. But it is the journey itself that counts! It is the experiences along the way that make you all who we are, that teach you the lessons you came to the earth dimension to learn, in order to evolve your immortal soul. But so many of you lose out on those very same experiences, simply because you are looking away! Not looking where you should be looking! Always looking to the future or hanging onto the past!

Dear ones, come back into living in the here and now! Come back and feel the passion that comes with living in the here and now. Come back and feel the sheer joy that comes with ***just being***! Look how the animals and birds live only in the here and now. That's how the birds can sing so much! That's how they can all fly so freely! That's how they can chirp and cheep! Have you ever seen a depressed bird flying about? Look at the trees and the mountains! The rivers and the lakes! Such grandeur! Such majesty! Such peace and serenity! And all they do is ***just be***!

I know you have to plan and organise a lot for your day-to-day lives. Of course I understand! Remember, I too was on the earth plane! I too had a certain amount of organisation to do! But the trouble in your world today is that so many of you have got caught up in the destructive, never ending cycle of going, going, going, getting, getting, getting, doing, doing, doing, so much so that you have no time to ***just be*** and allow yourself to enjoy just living in this moment in time, with no worries, no pressures, no restraints, just the sheer sublime feeling of ***being.***

Out of The Mind and Into The Heart

Is it not ironic that in your world today, unlike when I lived my life with Yeshua 2,000 years ago, you have so much machinery and all sorts of mechanised equipment which is supposed to make your life easier! But look what has happened! All that labour-saving equipment only seems to have freed most of you from certain forms of labour and forced you into working all the time in other forms of labour in order to pay for the life-style you are currently living! How has that happened?

That has all happened, dear ones, because your mind has been controlled by others who wish to make money from your desires for this and that and the other thing, promising you these things will bring you happiness, these things will make your life complete, these things are what you need, these things will bring you satisfaction! Guaranteed!

But you yourself know they do not deliver what has been promised! And you are caught, trapped in the rat race of commercialism, spending all your life working for money to buy the goods which will make those who control you into millionaires! And yes, I know you say that all this commercialism is creating jobs. But for what? To make so many things that humanity do not actually need? To make weapons and arms to kill? To produce artificial, processed, unnatural food to poison everyone and bring diseases and illness? To pollute all earth's waters to poison and kill? You are destroying the very source of your own natural abundance!

Your heart tells you the futility of all this! Your heart tells you that you can do with less. Your heart tells you that these things you work so hard and so long to accumulate are only transitory satisfactions. But your mind, your mind that has been taken over by others, is what you are still listening to!

If you can just come back into living in the **here and now**, as your **heart** keeps telling you, you will clearly see that everything you need is much more easily and readily available. The universe is an abundant place, with ample for everyone. But you seem to be unable to **trust** in the universe to supply your needs!

So **trust,** dear ones, is what I next wish to talk to you about!

With Love and Light!

I AM Mary Magdalene

CHAPTER 5:

COME BACK INTO TRUST

My dear ones!

Love and Light!

You have lost **trust**! You have lost **trust** in your beautiful abundant universe! You have lost **trust** in your beautiful abundant universe to deliver! And you have lost **trust** simply because you have been placing your **trust** in all the wrong places! Governments, churches, education institutions, monetary systems, legal institutions have all let you down so dreadfully and so catastrophically! The very ones in whom you placed your **trust** because you really believed they were looking after your best interests, guiding you, working for you, you now realise were only looking after their own interests, at your expense!

Do not beat yourself up over this! They have just been so devious, cunning and cleverly exploitive that they have conned you and manipulated your mind into handing over your power to them!

It is not too late! It is not too late for you to come back into **trusting** in the universe rather than in those who took over your power for their own mercenary gains!

You live in a beautiful, rich and abundant universe, where there is plenty for all. There is a Grand Design, a Grand Plan for your universe within the Oneness of the entirety of creation. You must *trust* in that divine plan. You seem to find it difficult to accept and *trust* that the universe is looking after you! You worry and fret over the most insignificant of things! Yes, the universe is looking after you in every tiny detail of your life, but you need to understand what part you yourself must perform in order to make the whole process work.

The universe is a reflection of yourself. The universe mirrors what you yourself send out to the universe through your thoughts, words and actions. In other words, you create your own reality! Yes, that is the power you have! But most of you see yourselves as victims, trapped in a chain of events beyond your control, a victim of circumstances which you cannot change.

You must understand, dear ones, that there is no such thing as chance or coincidence in your life. There is only synchronicity! Everything, absolutely everything is orchestrated within the universal natural laws.

And one of the most important universal laws is the law that governs giving and receiving, which goes hand in hand with the universal law of not just equal returns, but, indeed, the law of greater returns. This inviolable universal law concerning giving and receiving, in tandem with the law of greater returns, simply means that you must balance your giving and receiving, you must be able to give and receive in equal measures. And what you receive, or what is offered to you to receive, what you get back, is a direct result of what you yourself have given out.

When you send out thoughts or words of shortage, scarcity, want or poverty, the universe reflects that want and more of the same returns to you! That's why, my dear ones, you must be so careful with your thoughts and words. Your thoughts and words are energy, like everything else in creation, and once they leave you, they will manifest. Once you send your thoughts or words out, the universe immediately sets off a chain of events which brings your words or thoughts back to you.

And once you make your request to the universe, and once that set of synchronicities has been set in motion by the universe to get that request to you, you must step back and leave the universe to do ts job, the job that it does best, the job of delivering your request, that request placed by you with trust.

But so often you try and bring about your own outcome! And in doing so, you are upsetting and interfering with the universal flow of energy that has your request already on its way to you. You are blocking the universal energy, preventing the universal energy from delivering!

Your limited human vision cannot see the bigger or the whole picture. You do not know what is for your own highest good! You think you do! But the universe knows differently! The universe might not have the exact same car, or the exact same house, or the exact same job or whatever, on its way to you, but in fact something better! And the universe sends you multiple signs along the way that what you are going after through your own devices and under your own steam, is not suitable for you at all, and is therefore, not meant for you, your name is not on it! When you are experiencing difficulties and upsets along the way, then pay attention to those messages from the universe, pay attention to what the universe is telling you! For example, the mortgage plans falls through, the buyer has withdrawn, whatever upset there happens to occur, than that is a clear sign from the universe to stop interfering and let the universe get on with its job!

You must also learn to receive as well as to give. These must be in balance! Like all polarities! Your soul and the soul of everyone needs to give. But to whom can anyone give, if there is no person willing and happy to receive? By refusing another person's gift to you, whether in the form of a material gift or help or support of some kind or another, then you are denying that person the chance to feed their soul through the practice of giving. Understand? You must be able to receive as well as to give, in balance!

Trusting in the universe also means understanding another universal natural law. The law of non-attachment, or detachment!

People and material goods leave your life when they no longer serve your present purpose. You must be willing to let go and trust that others will enter who will serve you more purposefully. Do not let yourself get attached to material goods, for they are only transitory!

And you cannot get permanently attached to your children! You do not own them! They are not a possession! They too have a life plan to follow, just as you have your life plan to follow! You must free them to follow their own path! Let them fly! The universe is looking after them in just the same meticulous way it is looking after you! Your path is not their path! Your lessons are not their lessons! Your ways are not their ways! You cannot curtail their natural creativity or their natural expression or tendencies by imposing your own on them. This is their journey, not yours! When you disagree with their choices, the hardest thing to do is to do nothing! But that is exactly what you must do! No-thing! You must not judge or condemn them. Instead, you must shelve your big ego and allow them freedom to get on with it in their own way. Show them respect. When you interfere with your own opinions, when you declare judgement and condemnation, you are disrespecting them. Just remain on your own path, concentrate your energy and time there. That should be more than enough for you! Let the universe do its job in looking after your offspring! The universe knows what to do without you butting in!

This is all of what I mean by coming **back into trust**! Coming back into **trusting in the universe** to deliver for your **highest good** and the **highest good of all concerned**. **Trusting in the universe** to return to you in multi-fold what you give out. **Trusting in the universe** to take care of everything within the Grand Divine Plan.

If you have even the slightest worry over anything at all, then what does that mean? That slightest worry in which you are allowing yourself to indulge, means that you are failing to **trust in the universe**! You are failing to **trust** that the universe knows what is best for you, and will deliver. It may not be exactly what you want, because what you want may not be for the highest good of all concerned. But the universe will deliver that which is for the highest good of all concerned.

Even the slightest worry is coming from fear. The fear you feel is simply your ego trying to keep control of you. Letting your ego stay in the driving seat will make the world a threatening place for you. You need to shift from your ego-based mind into trusting in the universal God energy, allowing your natural essence, your own God essence, to take the driving seat. Choose to live your life through love and trust rather than through fear!

Remember, dear ones, that you yourself freely chose this current life you are now living. Your soul has made so many agreements with other souls at soul level before you came into this present incarnation. Nothing happens by chance, accident or coincidence, for there is no such thing! Everything is synchronised in order to serve your own chosen life purpose and plan. Often you rant and rave against what occurs in your life, your ego, as always, blocking your connection with Source, your ego making you doubt your own ability and worthiness. You need to look for the lesson in every incident, trusting in the fact that the universe has sent you this lesson in this particular form in order to fulfil your own freely chosen life plan.

So, my dear ones, **trust**! Just **trus**t! **Come back into trusting in the universe** to deliver for your own highest good and the highest good of all concerned, in every conceivable situation! Do not worry! The universe is looking after you, taking care of everything! When you are living in **trus**t, you have Spiritual power. The opposite to trust is doubt. And doubt comes from the ego. Do not, dear ones, let ego interfere! **Trust**, just as your heart urges you to do!

With Love and Light!

I AM Mary Magdalene

CHAPTER 6:

COME BACK INTO TRUTH

Dear ones!

Love and Light!

The only way you can be happy is if you are living your life in happiness and joy. Living your life in happiness and joy is your divine birth right! Living in happiness and joy is not something reserved for some and denied to others.

Unfortunately, many of you are still failing to accept this simple fact. Many of you still believe that you must suffer in order to achieve a raising of your Spiritual consciousness and that suffering will bring you closer to God. There it is again! That old belief that God is someone or something outside of yourself! But as I have already explained, **you yourself are God** in that you carry all the God elements **within yourself.** And as I have also explained before, the most important person in your life is you yourself. That does not mean being full of airs and graces, pursuing your own selfish self-centred aims, seeing yourself as above anyone else. It means looking after your own bodily and Spiritual needs above all else. Only then can you be of any assistance to anyone else.

Living in truth does not simply mean avoiding telling lies, or being totally honest, as many of you seem to think! Yes, you are right in the **totally honest** part! But what does **being totally honest** mean? **With whom** are you to be **totally honest**?

Well, as you are the most important person in your life, then is is not obvious that first of all you have got to be **totally honest and truthful** with yourself! You have first and foremost got to be **true to yourself**!

Being truthful and true to yourself means living the life that you yourself wish to live, acknowledging and accepting your own individual natural talents, creativity and inclinations. Very simple! But it saddens us to see so many of you not living your life as you wish. So many of you deny your own instinctive life course in order to please others, because you believe it is expected of you, or you will be disappointing to your parents or you will be letting other people down. That brings only anger, frustration and resentment in its wake!

It is sad to see so many of you denying your own inherent naure, living a lie, just to please someone else or because societal thinking dictates that you should do so. There are so many of you stuck in this soul-destroying situation!

So many of you are remaining in a broken and even violent marriage simply because of your children. Any relationship must serve both partners for that time. All relationships are speeding up, changing at this point in time, as the earth's vibrational energy force changes and speeds up. Time is speeding up, and therefore relationships are serving their purpose much more quickly than before. Contracts made at soul level are being fulfilled much more rapidly than before. Lessons are being learned much more rapidly than before. Can you see what is happening here? Your soul contract with that person has been fulfilled. That person no longer serves your life purpose. It is time to move on! You must release that person with love and gratitude for the lessons that person has taught you. And another will enter your life once you have completed this releasing of that which no longer serves you. Nothing or nobody in your life is permanent. And the only question you have to ask yourself is, am I happy in this situation? If the answer is no, than it is time to extricate yourself from that situation.

All sorts of contracts are coming to an end right now on your earth. And by trying to hold onto such contracts, you are blocking the natural flow of universal energy, restricting your freedom to move on and merge with energy similar to your own. Accept the winds of change which are blowing strongly right now throughout your entire planet, on both an individual level and on a collective level, transforming the energies all around you. Accepting these new energies is part of your life plan. New people and new experiences are coming your way, in synchronised movement, awakening you to your true nature, offering you the opportunity to learn the lessons you have freely chosen to learn during this life time. But you cannot accept the new until you release the old. It is fear, that old ego of yours again, that tells you to hold on, that tells you to wait until the storm has passed and everything will return to normal in your world. Dear ones, the very nature of life is change. Let go of that which is gone! Grab hold of that which is replacing all that is gone! You have not lost! You have gained! How can that be bad? Accept all the changes coming your way as a new day, a new direction in your life. Embrace change with an open heart and with gratitude.

More of you are living your life dictated by others, often parents, who wish you to follow in their footsteps, to be like them, to do as they do. But you are not like them! You are you! You are unique, with an inherent right to live according to all that your uniqueness entails! You and you only are responsible for your own soul evolution, and you must accept that responsibility fully. You and you only must find your own personal life path and carve out your own journey. Following someone else's agenda only leads to anger, hatred and resentment and hence to illness, suffering and pain.

Then there are those of you suffocating inside a body with which you do not feel at ease, a male trapped inside a female body, or a female trapped inside a male body. It is not a sin or an offence to be what your world society terms '*gay*'. That is simply a stigma attached to you by society and by the Church. But what is the norm? Is there a norm? Who has the right to say what or who is the norm? So many of you are struggling with your own sexuality, living in misery and fear, unable to express what to you feels natural. No person can judge another. No person has a right to judge another. Everyone is equal within the great universal God energy, everyone has an equal right to live as he or she chooses to live. And ironically, the reason why there are so many of you confused at this point in time over your sexuality is a direct result of how your so-called Christian Church has debased sex and the sacred sexual act for generations! That same Church which has castigated gay people so strongly, but which itself is so full of the same!

My dear ones, be not afraid to express your natural feelings, whatever your sexual tendencies. Each of you is working towards a balancing of your masculine and feminine energies within yourself, a reflection of Father/Mother God within each of you. And those amongst you whom society has termed gay, have maybe, indeed just managed to get nearer to that balance than those who continue to live in the limitation, in the limitation of the polarity of either one or the other. My beloved Yeshua was the perfect example of one who had balanced his masculine and feminine within himself. The perfected human being! Living in the limitless expansion of both rather that in the limitation of either one or the other.

Each of you is an expression of the creativity of the great universal God energy. A unique expression of that divine creativity! Not a copy! When you are expressing your uniqueness, you are expressing the great universal God energy in all its unlimited vastness. Each of your thoughts, words and actions expresses all the elements of the God essence. You are co-creating with God! But you have free will! You have a choice! You have a choice as to whether you use this power of co-creation with God for the good of mankind or for the detriment of mankind and your world. Before you choose, always listen to the wisdom within your own self, to the wisdom in your heart. Your heart will direct you to act through love. When you act through love, you are expressing the truth of God, and when you express the truth of God, you change your world.

So **coming back into truth** means living your life from your heart, as you yourself want to live it. It means being honest, first and foremost with yourself in every aspect of your life. If others cannot accept you as you are, then that is their problem, not yours! That is their lesson to learn, not yours! You are kindly and generously presenting them with an opportunity to learn a valuable lesson in order to evolve their soul. Whether they learn or not, that is their choice! But they will indeed learn it, if not in this life time, then in a future life!

Society tells you that you must all fall into line, all be the same, all follow the well trodden path. But how can that be? How can you all follow the same path, when you are all on a different journey? The path of your own soul is unique, the path that you yourself are creating is different from the path each other person is creating. And as you walk your own path, allow others to do the same. Do not block another's path by interfering in their life mission. Often when you think you are helping, you are actually in fact interfering, and that interfering comes from your ego, telling you that you know what is best for that person. When you interfere, you are merely meeting your own needs or acting out of fear.

Be proud of who and what you are! Express your own sexuality and your own creativity in the way that resonates with you yourself, as long as you are not hurting anyone else. Follow your *heart*! Follow your heart and let your soul fly freely to sing its own rapturous song within the harmony of the entire orchestra of *All That Is*!

With Love and Light!

I AM Mary Magdalene

CHAPTER 7:

COME BACK INTO YOUR INNER GODDESS

Dear ones!

Love and Light!

There is an inner Goddess within each of you! Unlock your inner Goddess and feel the exuberance, the passion, the enthusiasm with which you are meant to live your life. Many of you just wander aimlessly through life from day to day, just going through the motions, with no real passion or joy in what you are doing.

Unleashing your inner Goddess is reconnecting with your divine essence, and changing your life from the mundane and ordinary into the magical! And who amongst you does not want that? Unleashing your inner Goddess is an awakening of your Spirit, reminding you of the unlimited potential each and every one of you really and truly has!

As without, so within! Humanity has always yearned for and fought for freedom. You all have an inner Goddess, yearning for release, for freedom! Whimpering to be set free! But society has curtailed, stifled your inner Goddess, teaching you that life is all about responding to everyone else's demands and needs.

The masculine has been allowed to dominate in your world. And the result? A warring, fractious world, where so many of you live in fear, feeling lost, confused and so unhappy.

It is time for the return of the Goddess! And that is why I am here at this point in time, at the forefront of this movement, to restore the feminine to her rightful place in society, alongside the masculine, no longer subservient to it.

It is time for you all to cast off the beliefs and dictates of societal thinking and of your forefathers who created a patriarchal, male-dominated society, a society in which only the toughest could survive!

It is time to release your inner Goddess! Time to release your inner Goddess of passion, kindness, caring, nurturing, compassion, gentleness. Time to put yourself at the centre of your world. Time to see yourself as the most important person in your world. Time to speak your truth. Time to break the rules and beliefs of earlier generations. Time to balance the unbalanced. Time to live the life you have always dreamed of living, a life full of magic, freedom, happiness, and no longer a life of guilt, pain and suffocation. Time for each and every one of you to claim your power. Time for each and every one of you to reconnect with the feminine inside yourself and to realise how powerful that feminine power inside you truly is! A power that can transform your suffering world for the better, as you radiate your inner Goddess out all around you, spreading love and light, making everyone a winner! How different that is from what you have been taught! That wise, confident, radiant, feisty, spicy, nurturing, passionate and compassionate Goddess that lies within each of you waiting to be awakened, to be released into your world! Free at last to change your suffering world!

Let the transformation begin!

Come back into your inner Goddess!

With Love and Light!

I AM Mary Magdalene

CHAPTER 8:
COME BACK INTO NATURE

Dear ones!

Love and Light!

You are surrounded by so much beauty and magic in your world! Beauty is everywhere! Magic is everywhere! The manifestation of the creativity of the great universal God energy is everywhere! But many of you do not even notice. How sad for you that you are denying yourself this great pleasure, this great Spiritual indulgence!

You wish to escape from the frenzied world of every day living. Nature awaits you! You wish to escape from the pressures of your every day life. Nature awaits you! You wish to escape from fragmented living. Nature awaits you!

And many of you do not even notice!

Mother Nature is constantly calling out to you! Mother Nature is waiting to embrace you in loving arms of warmth and comfort! Mother Nature is waiting to heal and nourish your famished soul!

Yet many of you do not even notice!

Mother Nature is the embodiment of the creativity of the great Universal God energy. The great universal God energy finds such glorious expression in Mother Nature! Divine creativity at its most exotic, its most alluring, its most exuberant!

But many of you do not even notice!

Sadly, many of you are oblivious to all you are being offered. And not just oblivious. Mankind has encroached upon Nature's territory; mankind has destroyed; mankind has extracted; mankind has burned; mankind has exhausted and depleted all the natural resources that Mother Earth has so generously given, and continues to give.

There is an intelligence in all living things; God Intelligence. We are all part of an over-all, great collective Intelligence that seeks to express itself in many realities and in many forms. The beauty and the magnificence of creation is imbued into every life-form. Every rock and mountain, every river and ocean, every flower, every blade of grass, every tree and plant, every animal, bird and insect,- all are infused with the Spirit of God, all are intelligent forms of creation, resplendent in their uniqueness. And all with a greater understanding of their purpose than many of you on the earth have right now. All creatures have a job to do, all creatures have a soul purpose in being here. All are balancing and maintaining the great spirit of Mother Earth. People before you knew this better than you do. People before you knew how to respect Mother Earth and all on her. You must now return to ways of respect. Many of you have so severely limited yourselves by your denial of the existence of other forms of life around you, other than what you can perceive and experience with your five physical senses.

Nature is vibrant, pulsating, a living miracle, offering you love; teaching you lessons; giving you pleasure; healing you.

And for what does Nature ask in return? In return for all that

Nature gives you, Nature asks only for acknowledgement, respect and love. That's all! Ask for permission to enter Nature. Nature is the most natural place for you to be, but you are still a guest, tread softly and gently, observing and respecting the perfection around you.

It is through Nature that you can so easily access the divine! Nature is a channel through which God speaks to you! And many of your great writers, poets and artists have indeed heard and listened! And then they shared with you what they learned! But so many of you are not listening, caught up as you are in the deceiving allure of gross materialism and self-gratifying pursuits.

Nature is your greatest teacher. Nature holds the key to your uncerstanding of the meaning of life and death through the great yearly cycle of the seasons. You have forgotten your natural knowing of the rhythms and cycles of the earth and of all life-forms. All life-forms exist in a perpetual, on-going rhythm of cycles. Nature shows you how to go with the flow, to bend with the wind, to ride the storms, to grow towards the light. The flowers themselves nod and sway in time with the wind's gentle, carressing tune, perfectly harmonised. Nature teaches you to not worry, everything you need will manifest for you in a loving universe that knows your every desire and need, and will deliver. Yes, Nature has certainly given mankind much to think about!

What lessons your poets and artists all learned, what beauty they all saw in Nature! What peace and serenity they found there! What healing and nurturing they experienced!

Nature calls to you all! Nature is waiting to embrace you all in its healing balm; to cocoon you all in a gentle, soothing blanket of love and compassion; to enfold you all in a loving embrace, nurturing, replenishing, renewing; teaching you lessons; helping you all along your path; supporting you, encouraging you; and above all, healing you.

What a gift Spirit has given to you in Nature!

And all you have to do is accept and show appreciation for that gift; all you have to do is notice the splendour and beauty around you; all you have to do is respect the Elemental Kingdoms that co-exist alongside you on a different vibrational level, pouring their Spirit into the plants and flowers, the trees and the rivers. The Spirit that every living thing holds within it, the life-force that exists within all, animal, human, vegetable and mineral!

Dear ones, you are connected to Nature with an umbilical cord; but, unlike the umbilical cord that attaches the babe in the womb to the mother and is disconnected at birth, the umbilical cord that attaches you to Nature can never be disconnected or broken.

Remember how I earlier explained to you the natural universal law of greater returns? Well, that applies to Nature as to everything else. Whatever love you give to Nature, you will get all that returned to you again a hundred-fold! That's the natural universal law!

My dear ones, for your own good and healing, **come back into Nature**!

Love and Light!

I AM Mary Magdalene

CHAPTER 9:

COME BACK INTO YOUR OWN SPIRITUAL LIGHT

Dear ones!

Love and Light!

You have a song that says:

'Shine your light for everyone to see', and when you shine your light, *'You'll overlook the blindness of the narrow minded people on the narrow minded streets'*.

Another of your songs says:

'Let your light shine', and *'If you could see you the way I see you, you'd start flying on your own.'*

Yes, dear ones! If only you could see yourselves as we in the Spirit worlds see you! If only you could see your shining bright light as we see it!

Dear ones, you have come from the Light, and it is to the Light you will return. You carry the Light with you and within you at all times.

Let your light shine! Let your light show! You are unique! You are one of a kind! It is time to realize who and what you are! It is time to step into your unique greatness!

You are of the great God essence, shimmering in your splendour! Sparkling in your magnificence! Awesome in your greatness! Unlimited in your potential!

You are beautiful! There is only one you! You have a unique job to do while you are on planet earth. No one else can do your job, in just the same way as you cannot do anyone else's job either! The job you yourself chose to do before you entered your present incarnation, the job you and you only can do!

In your daily life, shine your light out to everyone you meet! You never know the effect your light will have on others! When those who live in darkness, in the absence of the Light, see your shining Light, they are drawn to you like the moth to the flame! They are drawn to realise that there is somewhere else for them to exist rather than in the debilitating darkness where they now find themselves. And it is your bright, shining sacred Light of your soul that will light up the path for them. It is your bright, shining, sacred soul-light that will rescue them from the misery of existence in darkness.

So let your Light shine! But before you can let your Light shine, you have to remember that you have that shining bright light within you!

You **ARE** a shining bright light!

Keep saying to yourself: *'This little light of mine, I'm going to let it shine!'*

Continue to let your Light shine! Let it shine, let it shine, let it shine...............

Energy always follows the intention.

So come **back into your own Spiritual Light**!

Love and Light!

I AM Mary Magdalene

CHAPTER 10:

COME BACK INTO LOVE

Dear Ones!

Love and Light!

So many of you continue to look outside of yourself for **Love**!

God is **Love**! God is **Love** or primordial energy. God is **All That Is**. Therefore **Love** is **All That Is**.

God encompasses everything. Therefore **Love** encompasses everything. There can be nothing outside of God. Therefore there can be nothing outside of **Love**.

And you? You are of the God Essence! You are all the elements of God. Therefore you **are Love**!

So if you **are Love**, then you do not need to search for or to find **Love**, because you yourself **are Love**, in just the very same way that you do not need to search for God! You are God! You **are Love**! The power of **Love** is the power of God, because God is **Love**. It has nothing to do with the way you feel about someone.

Love is a state of being. A state of being devoid of fear. Fear is the polarity of **Love**. **Love** is all there is. There can be nothing else. God is **Love**. They are one and the same thing. You are **Love**. You came from **Love** and you will return to **Love**. As a divine creation, you are **Love incarnate**.

Breathe **Love** in with every breath you take. Spirit is breath. Spirit is **Love**. **Love** is breath. Allow **Love** to expand with each breath through your heart and over your entire being. With each out-breath spread this **Love** to all you meet.

There can only be one kind of **Love**. There can only be ***unconditional Love***.

And what is ***unconditional Love***? Unconditional **Love** means accepting every person, and yourself, as the beautiful Spiritual being, the shining Spiritual Light that you and they are. And because you see yourself and everyone else as that pure Light, the Essence of God, then you do not judge, you do not criticise, you do not condemn. You send them only Love and Light, refusing to get involved in any negative attribute such as hatred, jealousy or anger. And you do not harbour feelings of guilt with yourself.

Unfortunately, most of you still see **Love** as something conditional. You tell your loved ones you will love them if they do this or that or the other thing to please you. You tell yourself you will love yourself when you do this or that or the other thing. That is not **Love**! That is gross manipulation!

And gross manipulation is the greatest cancer in your world today!

Yeshua did not wish to form any sort of religion. Yet his teachings have been used by egos as a means of control for the last 2,000 years. The ancient teachings, and Yeshua's teachings had but one aim, to connect humanity with God. But look what has happened! Religions have been used as power tools, to make humanity dependent on them for access to God, for access to their own divine nature.

Out of The Mind and Into The Heart

The Christian religion and other religions teach about **Love**. But it is not **Love** in its real meaning about which they are teaching! How can it be? How can they be teaching about the real meaning of **Love** when they have murdered and tortured those who do not share their beliefs and accept their teachings? How is that **Love**? That is simply controlling through fear.

Forgiveness was a very important teaching of Yeshua. To forgive is to l ve in the Oneness of the great universal energy that is God. Forgiveness is to live in **Love**. Forgiveness is a sacred practice. It is a practice of the heart, not of the mind. When you forgive, you raise your Spiritual vibration, you come into wholeness. When you forgive, you relieve yourself of that burden you were carrying like a ton weight around your neck. And remember! All is One! We are all One! So when you forgive someone, you are forgiving yourself for having maybe done that same thing in a previous life-time! When you forgive, you are recognising that person as yourself.

As above, so below. When you pass over back to the Spirit world at the end of your current life-time, there will be no judgement or condemnation. There is only **Love**. **Unconditional Love**. No one judges you. No one condemns you. No one punishes you. You simply review your own life-time and consider whether you learned the lessons you came into this incarnation to learn, or whether you did not. Your ego will not be at your life review! Only your soul! Nothing will be hidden! All will be bared! All will be bared in **Love**.

There is an ancient Hawaiian Mantra that has been used by the Kahuna, the mystic healers, for centuries. It is very beautiful. It is called '**HO'OPONOPONO**'. Let me remind you of the words and how it works!

Just close your eyes and imagine anyone or any situation where you are having difficulty or experiencing trouble. Repeat these simple four phrases, with prayerful intention:

I AM SORRY

PLEASE FORGIVE ME

I LOVE YOU

THANK YOU

Your intention is the key here, and indeed intention is the key to everything. Your intentions are like magnets. Your intentions are energy. Energy follows your intentions. They draw back to you what you send out. The more you declare your intention, the more you believe in it, then the more easily your intention will be fulfilled.

Dear ones, remember, **LOVE IS ALL THERE IS**!

Love is God.

You are Love.

Come back into Love!

Love and Light!

I AM Mary Magdalene

CHAPTER 11:

RETURN OF THE GODDESS

Dear ones!

Love and Light!

It is time for the Goddess to return to your world!

So who or what is the Goddess? The Goddess is the Divine Feminine, the Divine Mother, the source of all life. Males do not gve birth, only females. That is the natural order of all things. All women have a natural healing ability, because by their very nature they are life-givers, nurturers and nourishers.

Your far ancestors all knew that all life comes from woman and the feminine, so they honoured and revered the Great Mother as the creator of all. They knew beyond any doubt whatsoever that everything comes from Mother Earth, absolutely everything! Mother Earth is the constant unfailing supply of all we need and have. The Milky Way! The name for the heavens! Where do you think that name came from? The source of the Mother's Milk! She who nurtures and nourishes all!

All the great Spiritual cultures and traditions your world has ever known, all the great wisdoms, all the great ancient teachings and mysteries, all of these were spawned in the ancient cultures of Egypt, India and China. From there, they seeped downwards and in turn permeated the great teachings, beliefs and practices of the

Mayans, the Druids, the Magi, the Essenes, the Greeks, the Therapeutae, the Native American Indians and the Gnostic Christians.

And in those early cultures of Egypt, India and China, it was the Mother God who was revered and honoured, simply because the Mother God, the Divine Feminine was recognised and acknowledged as the source and giver of all life.

So how come your present world has ceased to honour the Cosmic Mother, the same Cosmic Mother, the same Divine Mother that was revered in cultures around your world long before the patriarchal gods were even born?

What has happened? What has happened in your world to make it the unbalanced place it now is? A world where the masculine, not the feminine, rules the roost? A world where wars, aggression, hatred, violence, fear and anger are all the norm? A world where the erstwhile peace, abundance and joy which went hand in hand with respect and reverence for the feminine no longer exists?

Your Christian Church bible has taught you that man, Adam was created first! And then Eve was created from Adam. How can that be? Dear ones, can you not see what has happened here? It was the early so-called Christian Church, called into existence by Emperor Constantine three centuries after Yeshua and I left the earth plane, that began the world wide religion of Christianity. Constantine's motivation in creating Christianity was political, and only political, his sole purpose being to bring unity to the vast Roman Empire. That early Christianity had nothing to do with Yeshua and everything to do with political Roman power and dominance.

Yeshua and I lived in a Roman occupied Palestine. The majority of people followed the Judaic religious rules and beliefs. Part of those beliefs were the subservience of women in a patriarchal society. Jesus taught contrary to this belief. That's why he made so many enemies and ended up being crucified. He treated women and men equally. He respected the Divine Feminine. And he learned all this during his time in the great Mystery Schools in Egypt and India, during the years that your gospels have failed to account for his whereabouts.

The great Ancient Mystery Schools taught the secrets of the natural cycles of Mother Nature, and how everything moves in a cycle, mirroring the cyclical movement of Mother Earth herself. When we move in tandem with the natural rhythms of Mother Nature we are moving in this sacred circle, linked to the pulse, the heart-beat of the entire cosmos. Your early ancestors knew the importance of the circle and the natural on-going cycles of Nature. That is evident in their religious sites such as Stonehenge. Within this circle, within the natural cycle of Nature, there is no dominance of any sort whatsoever. All moves in harmony.

The Goddess teaches the path of the heart. The path of the heart teaches that all life is sacred and that we are all part of the great Universal Intelligence that moves through all things. The path of the heart teaches that you must honour the living energies that underpin all forms of life in the entire cosmos. And the path of the heart teaches that each and every one of you is entirely responsible for your own Spiritual development. Each of you is entirely responsible for deciding what or who the Divine is for you, and forming a meaningful relationship with that Divine Presence.

The Goddess has been known by various names throughout history and throughout many diverse cultures. In ancient Egypt she was known as Isis, and for over seven thousand years was worshipped in temples across your entire world. Isis was the great queen, the faithful devoted wife of Osiris, the courageous fearless mother of Horus. She was the healer, the holder of wisdom and knowledge, and founder of the Egyptian Mystery Schools. She combined the roles of mother, daughter, sister, lover, teacher, and guardian and keeper of wisdom. And it was in the Egyptian Mystery Schools and in the Temple of Isis in Egypt, that both Yeshua's mother, known then as Mary Anna, and myself were both trained as priestesses.

In Christianity, the Goddess is called Mother Mary, the great Mother of compassion; in Judaism, she is known as Sophia, the Goddess of Wisdom; in Japan and India as Lakshmi, the Mother of Generosity and in China, where her statues are everywhere, she is embodied as Quan Yin, the protector of children.

And it is in myself, Mary of Magdala, that the Goddess Isis has continued to be honored for the last 2,000 years. I was the Spiritual partner, the Spiritual equal of Yeshua, the female aspect of the Christ, deprived of my status by the male-dominated patriarchal Christian Church. Yeshua entrusted the inner teachings of the greater Mysteries to me, but those early Christian Church fathers could not accept that. Nor could they accept that Mary Anna, Yeshua's mother, was trained as a priestess in the Temple of Isis in Egypt. So how did they deal with us? They elevated Mary Anna to the role of Virgin Mother, the epitome of passivity, subservience, obedience and acceptance. But Mary Anna was a strong, independent woman, strongly versed in the ancient Mysteries and the teachings of the ancient Mystery schools and very much an influence in Yeshua's life. She was of both Celtic and Hebrew ancestry, and her name, Mary Anna was after her mother, Anna, the grand-mother of Yeshua and the great strong matriarchal influence in all our lives. But as a woman, Yeshua's mother, being that strong, influential person in Yeshua's life, was unacceptable as such to the early Church fathers!

And me? How did they deal with me? They castigated me as a prostitute, whore and a sinner, possessed by seven demons. But I was none of these!

And what about the only other woman featured in your Christian Church bible? Eve! How did they portray Eve? As the evil one, the temptress of the man Adam, the one who caused him to give into temptation and hence brought about the fall of man!

The days of the Goddess were lived in honoring the natural cycles of Nature. But the Christian Church has re-written her history. The Christian Church has hidden the Divine Mother from your modern world. The Christian Church has removed the Goddess of love and replaced her with their God of fear. The Christian Church has established a male God, somewhere above the clouds, outside of yourself, separate and divorced from what is happening on your planet earth. And look at the result! Mankind has desecrated and exploited the earth's stores of abundance simply because mankind does not see God on or in your earthly dimension. What a difference from the times when civilizations saw God in every plant, every blade of grass, every animal, every living thing! Then there was respect and reverence for Mother Nature, for Mother

Eileen McCourt

God!

The Christian Church has taken over all those ancient Goddess sites, all those Spiritual sites where Mother Nature was revered and honored, and because they knew well the importance and significance of such sites, built as they were along the energy ley-lines of your earth, in total harmony with the natural cycles of Mother Earth, those early Christian Church fathers made those sacred sites their own and built their churches and cathedrals over those same spots. Hence they were able to harness the natural sacred energies there for their own power, and rename those sacred sites in their new, fabricated religion that they called Christianity. They renamed the Goddess to suit their own purpose and moved the natural sacred holy days of the year celebrated by those whom they came to denigrate as 'pagan' cultures. The Goddess Brigit, for example, that great Goddess of the Celtic world, was changed into Saint Bridget by your early Church fathers, greatly devaluing her original identity. She was given the title *'saint'*, putting her in the same category as all those other *'saints'* established by the Christian Church, some simply because they had been a pope in their life-time!

Dear ones, surely you can now see what has happened? Surely you can now see more clearly how your world has changed from a world where the great Mother God, the Divine Feminine was revered and honoured as the great life-giver and nourisher, to a world where Father God, that great punishing male, judges and condemns you all to a life of eternity in either the fires of hell or rewards you with eternal life in the paradise of heaven.

Yes! It is time for the return of the Goddess! How will you

recognise her? Let me explain!

The entire cosmos is made up of polarities, which are opposites. Each of these polarities has a masculine and a feminine expression of itself. Male and female. Man and woman. Polarities. Opposites. You must move away from these polarities and find the balance between the two. You must find the balance between the feminine aspects and the masculine aspects, and when that balance is achieved, there is harmony. When you move away from that balance, there is only senseless suffering and violence. Your world, unfortunately for all of you, has been unbalanced for the last 2,000 years and more. Too much masculine and a deficit of feminine!

Each of these masculine and feminine polarities has, in turn, both a positive and a negative side to it. The masculine has shown itself too much in its negative side. That is the side to the masculine which is brutal, competitive, punishing, abusive, warlike, angry, revengeful, seeking dominance, power and subservience from the feminine. On the other hand, the positive side of the masculine is that which displays courage, wisdom, love, tolerance, bravery, leadership, understanding, willingness to help, desire to protect, equality, consideration for the needs and feelings of others, bravery to act on convictions, building, doing, taking chances for the good of others, sacrificing for the good of others, championing the truth, serving the good of the community. What a difference! Truly knights in shining armour!

And so it is with the feminine! The positive side of the feminine is that which shows caring, nurturing, healing, devotion and faithfulness, forgiving, understanding, compassion, service to the needs of others, passion, tenderness, love. On the other hand, the negative side to the feminine is that which shows itself in gossip, jealousy, anger, desire for revenge, neediness, dependency, manipulation, cunning, deceit, exploiting sexuality for personal gains, with-holding sex as a form of punishment or showing displeasure.

And there is one thing to which you must pay attention in all of this!

When the female is shown respect, love and appreciation, secure in the knowledge that she is appreciated and valued and protected, then she responds with complete commitment, creativity and devotion, willing to please and to better others. The positive aspects of the masculine, when applied, take out the best in the female. But when the masculine negative attributes are felt by the feminine she reacts with the negative aspects within her own nature, resorting to those negative aspects for her own survival and the survival and well-being of her children.

Dear ones, do you understand what I am saying here? It is the positive attracting the positive and the negative attracting the negative in the masculine and the feminine energies. Negative begets negative. Positive begets positive. It is the law of attraction! And you all have the potential to express all four of these aspects. You can all be too aggressive, too bullying, too demanding, too loud, too intrusive. Like wise, you can all be too laid-back, too unmotivated, too lazy, too passive, too frightened to take the appropriate action.

You must all balance your inner masculine with your inner feminine. These polarities are not in competition! They should complement each other and further each other for the good of all. Look at it like this. The feminine is the metaphorical queen, in touch with her heart, in touch with Source. The masculine is her knight in shining armour, her warrior, whose main purpose is to bring to fruition her dreams and aspirations, and without whom those dreams will never be realised. She is the one with the dreams, coming from her intuition, he is the one she needs to bring those dreams to reality for the good of all. The two must work together, side by side, as equal partners, each contributing to the whole in response to the call from the other.

And this has all been portrayed in what you call your Fairy Tales. Those stories are not just meant to bring delight and magic to your young children! They are meant for all of you! There are messages in there! Messages which most of you have until now failed to get!

Think of '**Snow White**'! What is that fairy tale about? It is about the evil of a female, called the Wicked Queen, who is trapped in the negative feminine polarity. Her antithesis is Snow White, the positive feminine polarity, who has fled from the evil envy of the Wicked Queen. But for Snow White to be saved, she must be awakened by her heroic prince. The positive feminine attribute must be merged with the masculine positive attribute. Only then will the two be united in love and live happily ever after.

Think too of '**Cinderella**'! Here you have again, the negative feminine polarities of greed, envy and ambition which have taken over the three Ugly Sisters. The unfortunate victim of this, Cinderella, can only be saved in her misfortune by being courageous enough to be seen at the grand ball by the noble prince, who nobly searches for her to follow the instincts of his heart and delve beyond surface appearances. When the two find each other, the prince marries her, and restores her to the throne as his equal, both of them living happily ever after.

And don't forget '***Sleeping Beauty***'! The princess can only be brought back to life by the noble prince who has the courage to search for her. Her kingdom is frozen in time, she represents the sleeping spirit hidden inside each one of you, which can only be awakened by your positive other half.

These fairy tales all end in happily ever after. And why? Simply because the positive attributes in the male hero have merged with the positive attributes in the female heroine, manifesting love, peace and harmony for all concerned. The message is that for you to come into balance, you need to embrace both sides of yourself, the masculine and the feminine, and you need to embrace the positive of each, for that is what brings out the best in all.

And this is what was meant by Yeshua's teachings of '***The Way***'. The balance inside each of you of the masculine and feminine energies, marking a path of wholeness, integration and Oneness. The way to Enlightenment! The way to the perfected human being!

And this interaction of these various dance movements between the masculine and feminine forces is all not just played out at a personal level, but also at a global level, through religions, institutions and societies. There are political regimes that bully, coerce and dominate through instilling fear, oppression, threats and punishments, just as there are also religions that bully and control their members through fear and guilt. All of these are caught, trapped in the negative masculine polarity! And the result?

Out of The Mind and Into The Heart

Everyone suffers!

So now, dear ones, do you understand why I tell you that it is essential for the Divine Feminine, the Goddess to return to your world?

The Goddess, with all the intuition, all the Spiritual connection with Source, all the dreams for a wonderful world where everyone knows only peace, joy, abundance and happiness! But the Goddess alone cannot manufacture it! She needs her knight in shining armour, her warrior, who can share the dream, to bring it into reality for her, and then they will both live happily ever after. The positive attributes of the feminine, the Goddess, have been merged with the positive aspects of the masculine, responding to her call, making her feel loved, cherished, valued and respected. And when the female feels like that, the male responds by feeling valued, honoured and appreciated for the contribution he has made, and which he was happy to make.

This return of the Goddess is happening right now in your world. And I, Mary Magdalene, am at the spear-head of this movement. I am here to help further this balancing which will bring peace to your troubled world.

Your world can be returned to a world without bloodshed or war! Your world can see an end to conflict and suffering. But first you all need to understand and accept that the way to achieve all this dream, and this dream can indeed be achieved, is not through masculine dominance at the expense of the feminine. It can only be achieved, as it was before, and so it can be again, by the equal merging of the masculine and the feminine. It can only be achieved by the acceptance of the equality of Father/Mother God, and not a male, punishing God. This masculine dominance, belief in a single, male dominating, punishing God over the last 2,000 years, the age of Pisces, has led only to conflict, duality and separation. Can you not see how this has failed you, dear ones? But now, with the dawn of this new age of Aquarius, everything is possible! The winds of change are unstoppable! Controlling religions are losing their grip on your souls! You are ready to accept the return of the Goddess!

You are ready to honour Mother Earth once again, simply because you now see Mother Earth as the source of all your needs. You are ready to live in Oneness once again simply because you now see that there is no separation, we are all one, what you do to another, you do to yourself!

You are ready to respect and honour all forms of life on your beautiful planet earth, simply because you now realise that they too have their purpose and mission in being in your world. And the animals are not on planet earth to be slaughtered for profit or for sport or entertainment!

You are ready to respect Mother Nature, simply because you now understand that you must live your lives in tune with the great cycles of Nature, because you are all part of that great cycle of universal energy. And you now know that Mother Nature teaches you your greatest and most important lessons!

You are indeed ready to break out, to break free, of the trap that you have been in for so long now, the trap of materialism, fear and self-doubt, imposed upon you by those who are greedy and lustful for money and power.

You are ready to re-connect with your own God essence, ready to form your own personal relationship with your own Divine Presence, and to no longer accept without question the dogmas, doctrines and teachings of a patriarchal religion that claims to be built on the teachings of Jesus, but is most clearly not!

You are ready to cast off the controlling of your soul by others for their own gains, and take back responsibility for your own soul development and evolution.

You are ready for the ***return of the Goddess***!

All is well, dear ones! All is as it should be!

Love and Light!

I AM Mary Magdalene

Eileen McCourt

CONCLUSION

FROM MY HEART TO YOURS:

Live your life with passion

Dear Ones,

Love and Light!

It is with such great joy that we in the higher dimensions watch those of you who have a passion for what you do! When you live your life with passion, the light that shines from within you is truly beautiful! When you are advancing your soul path, you are shining your soul Light for everyone to see. That beautiful shining light is lit by your emotions and your feelings, which in turn are generated by your feeling heart. Your heart is not a stone! Your heart is not cold! Your beautiful heart knows only love, truth and compassion.

This is a time of rapid parting of the veils between the Spirit worlds and the physical world and a time of increasing chaos in your earthly world. Everything is changing! You need to embrace these rapid changes and not block these new emerging energies that are here to raise your vibration to a new, higher level than ever before in the history of humanity.

And in order to be able and ready to embrace these new energies you need to let go! You need to let go and, having let go, you are then able to experience! That is what being God truly is! An experience! So you must experience all that you can during this current life-time.

Let go of your ego, your mind, and experience **living from your heart**.

Let go of everything outside of yourself and **experience living in your own body**.

Let go of separation and individualism and experience **Oneness** and **wholeness**.

Let go of everything you thought you were and experience **what you really are**, a Spiritual being having a physical experience for this life-time.

Let go of everything you think you have to be and experience **what you want to be**.

Let go of everything everyone else wants you to be and experience what your own **heart wants you to be**.

Let go of doing and going and experience **just being**.

Let go of trying and experience **just knowing**.

Let go of living in the past or in the future and experience living in the **here and now**.

Let go of worry and experience living in **trust**.

Let go of pretending and experience living in **truth**.

Let go of fear and experience living in **love**.

Let go of what you think you own and experience **freedom and detachment**.

Let go of numbness and experience **sensuality**.

Let go of want and scarcity and experience **over-flowing abundance**.

Let go of dis-ease and experience **health**.

Let go of limitation and experience **limitless abundance** and **endless possibilities**.

Let go of the desire for recognition and experience **confidence and security**.

And when you have let go of everything that no longer serves you, when you surrender to All THAT IS, you will indeed experience **true peace and happiness**.

Know that you are divinely guided in all you do. That's because you are of divine essence. When expressing yourself, repeat over and over again until you really feel it, until you really live it:

I am love.

I am divine essence.

I am the Light.

I am Source.

I am unique.

I am divine expression

I am bountiful.

Eileen McCourt

I am awake.

I am being.

I am flowing.

I am forgiving.

I am growing.

I am healthy.

I am genuine.

I am knowing.

I am magnificent.

I am grateful.

I am miraculous.

I am nurturing.

I am compassion.

I am beautiful.

I am unconditional.

I am whole.

I am timeless.

I am eternal.

I am infinite.

Out of The Mind and Into The Heart

I am perfect.

I am truth.

I am unlimited.

I am enlightened.

I am incarnate.

I am radiance.

I am complete.

I am bountiful.

I am fulfilled.

I am the wind.

I am the sky.

I am the sunset.

I am the dawn.

I am within.

I AM.

I AM THAT I AM THAT I AM.

Dear ones, we in the Spiritual worlds applaud and honour you for what you are doing. You are fast-tracking your soul evolution in these times of uncertainty, upheaval and turmoil. You are doing what you volunteered to do. You are fulfilling what you showed up to do.

Continue to ask us for guidance and assistance. Continue to watch for the signs we are constantly sending you. Continue to live from your heart. Continue to live in joy and happiness, as you are meant to live. Remember, you are divine essence! You are unlimited in your potential! You are co-creators with the great universal God energy. Use your power wisely and with compassion.

I send you unlimited love from my heart to your heart. Feel my hand on your heart. Feel your hand on my heart. Feel your heart beat in tandem with mine and with all creation. Know that we are all One. Know that Yeshua and I will never leave you or desert you. We will continue to guide you until you are all back with Source, until we are all together again in the great universal energy, the great universal Light of Source.

I send you Love and Light.

I AM Mary Magdalene.

Out of The Mind and Into The Heart

Eileen McCourt

Printed in Poland
by Amazon Fulfillment
Poland Sp. z o.o., Wrocław